The Engli

Tales from History, Le   .....ore

British Library Cataloguing in Publication Data
A catalogue record for this book is available from the British Library

ISBN 0 9522098 3 7

First published in Great Britain in 1996 by:-

P3 Publications
13 Beaver Road, Carlisle, Cumbria
CA2 7PS

Printed in Great Britain by
The Amadeus Press Ltd.
Cleckheaton
BD19 4TQ

Introduction

The material for this book comes from a variety of sources. Much of it is based on information provided by the early guide writers on the Lake District such as John Gilpin, 1772 and Harriet Martineau 1855, to mention but two. These early guide books give a fascinating insight into the awe and esteem that visitors to this wild land of mountains had for the area. The more recent history and other information was derived from a variety of sources, including interviews with local inhabitants, who remember the Lake District of their youth. I would like to take this opportunity to give an extra thank you to those many people who talked to me and provided local titbits of information, which were invaluable in aiding my researches

David Ramshaw
Carlisle, March 1996

Acknowledgements

I would like to gratefully acknowledge the help given by many individuals and organisations during the preparation of this book.

Stephen White and his colleagues of Carlisle Library Service deserve special mention for their patience and help in finding books and documents for me from the Local History Collection.

In addition my grateful thanks go to Carlisle Library Service for permission to use selected drawings and photographs from old books. The staff of Carlisle Record Office for their valuable assistance. John Adams for much of the mining information. Anne Bowman for help with Wythop local history. W R Hartland for information on the Embleton Sword. Dave Lush for his drawings. Sid Robinson for information on the Blencathra crosses. Ursula Banister for information on Mary Harrison. Lyndsey Barker for permission to use material from Mabel M Barker's 'Memoirs of my first leader'. John Storey for his coat of arms. Mackay Design Associates for the Trailbarrow photograph. Norman Nicholson for the Millican Dalton photograph. Finally I have made great efforts to contact members of the family of Nicholas Size, author of 'The Secret Valley', unfortunately without success. I have made use of material from Nicholas' book, written in the 1930's, in my description of the Battle of Rannerdale and acknowledge that source with thanks.

Buttermere in 1819, looking round Rannerdale Point

3

Contents

Haweswater and Mardale

Ullswater, Glenridding, Patterdale
Martindale, Hartsop and Kirkstone Pass

Patterdale - Helvellyn - Grasmere

Borrowdale & The Derwent Fells

Contents Contd..
Caldbeck, Mosedale, Mungrisedale and Threlkeld

Bassenthwaite, Braithwaite, Embleton and Lorton

Buttermere, Crummock and Loweswater

Pocklington's Island on Derwentwater   Joseph Pocklington 1786

The Border Reivers

The Border Reivers or Raiders brought a new word to the English language during the Middle Ages. In their raids on their neighbours in the *'debatable lands'* they stole cattle, raped, pillaged and *'bereaved'* many a wife and family of their husband and father. These eastern fells provided corridors south for the marauding Scots and there are many tales of battles and skirmishes among these hills. Great Scarth Pass, Nan Bield Pass and High Street were frequently used.

One such story describes how the burghers of Kendal received warning of an imminent Scottish raid. The raiders were expected to pass through Mardale by either Great Scarth or Nan Bield Pass. The men of Kendal laid a trap, posting their archers among the rocky ground on and surrounding Castle Crag on the west bank of Haweswater. When within shooting distance, the bowmen of Kendal poured volley after volley of arrows into the raiders killing them all. The Scots were buried where they fell. The archers of Kendal were famed for their bravery. Besides covering themselves with glory at Agincourt they featured in the battle of Flodden Field:

'These were the bows of Kendale bold
Who fierce will fight and never flee'

Incidentally, Castle Crag was probably no stranger to such violent happenings, like its namesake in Borrowdale, it is the site of an iron age fort.

Pack Horse Route from Kendal via Longsleddale, Great Scarth (*Gatesgarth*) Pass
and Mardale to Penrith
(from an old print)

The Corpse Road and Mardale Church

Prior to 1728, when Mardale Church was granted a licence for burials, baptisms and marriages, anyone who died in the dale had to be transported via the old corpse road to the parish church of Shap. The corpse road wends its way across the northern slopes of Selside Pike down into Swindale Head. The dead were strapped to the backs of fell ponies for the trip, as the route is rather a rough fell path and quite unsuitable for wheeled vehicles.

A story has been handed down of one such journey when a wicked man, who had died in Mardale with an undivulged crime, was being carried over to Shap on the back of a strong young horse. During the journey a dreadful thunderstorm arose and the terrified horse bolted. For three months it roamed the fells evading every attempt at capture. Then, as is usual in such tales, the secret came to light, the horse allowed itself to be caught and the poor man was buried at Shap where, hopefully, he rests in peace.

The last body to be born over the fells for burial at Shap was John Holme of Brackenhow on 17th June 1736. The first burial in Mardale churchyard was that of John Turner in 1731. Of course since then, as a result of the water scheme, the bodies at Mardale have been exhumed and re-buried, the majority of them at Shap. The church has been demolished and some of its fittings distributed to other churches in the county. The bell went to St.Barnabas,Carlisle, where it can still be heard today. The weather vane and various other artefacts went to Shap and the pulpit to Borrowdale. The stonework of the windows can still be seen, as it was incorporated into the upper chamber of the water intake well on the eastern shore of the lake.

Mardale Church (before the flood)

7

High Street - thoroughfare and meeting place

High Street probably derives its name from the '*strata*' or Roman road which, following the course of an earlier British track, leads along its ridge at more than 2000 ft above sea level. In the Middle Ages this path was used by the Border Reivers on their forays into the district and was known as 'The Scots Rake.'

This rather inhospitable place was surprisingly well frequented by the local inhabitants in times gone by. Over 150 years ago, on holidays and feast days, horse race meetings were held on the broad flat top above Blea Water. Hence the name Racecourse Hill. Clarke in his 'Survey of the Lakes,' describes how, on the 10th of July each year the shepherds of the area assembled here for:

'horse racing, wrestling, and other such like country diversions: hither, likewise, every one brings the stray sheep he has found during the preceding year, that they may be owned: they also at this time amuse themselves with fox hunting.'

He goes on to describe how at one such hunting a man called Dixon fell about 1000 ft from the top of Blea-Water Crag. Although he hit the rocks several times on his way down, he had no broken bones, but was terribly bruised and was almost completely scalped. Dixon, a resident of Kentmere, survived to tell the tale and Clarke visited him many years afterwards. Clarke relates that, the only hair on his head was a small tuft above one ear. The place on the crag where this unfortunate event occurred became known as Dixon's Three Jump.

Horse Racing on High Street more than 150 years ago
(from an old print)
Blea-water Crag is in the foreground

8

Mardale, the drowned valley

It is now over 50 years since Manchester Corporation, in its thirst for water, flooded the Mardale valley and ended a way of life for ever. The inhabitants were moved out and the hamlet of Mardale, farmsteads, pub, church and field walls were demolished.

Lying as it does on the old packhorse route from Kendal towards Penrith by way of Longsleddale and Gatesgarth Pass, this remote corner of lakeland had been inhabited for hundreds if not thousands of years. Its inhabitants had survived the rigours of severe winters, the harassment of border raiders and other natural and manmade calamities only to be eventually vanquished by Manchester Corporation.

As in Patterdale one family settled and remained in the valley for generations. According to tradition one Hugh Holme arrived in the valley in 1208. He was fleeing from the vengeance of King John after the failure of the Canterbury conspiracy and concealed himself in a cave in Riggindale; known as Hugh's Cave to this day. By long ownership of property and by residence at Chapel Hill his descendants became known as *'The Kings Of Mardale.'* The last male Holme was Hugh Parker Holme who died in 1885 aged 34. The last person with the name Holme to live in the valley was his aunt, Mrs T Holme, who died in 1915 aged 90.

In 1919 the Manchester Corporation obtained parliamentary sanction to convert Haweswater into a reservoir. By 1925 they had bought out the landowners and taken possession of the land around the lake. However preparation and construction took a further sixteen years. The reservoir was brought into service in October 1941 and overflowed for the first time in December 1942.

Hugh Parker Holme

The last King of Mardale and sole male
survivor of a long line, commencing with
Hugh Holme in the year 1208

Mardale, the drowned valley

The dam raised the level of Haweswater by 96 ft, trebling its surface area and increasing its capacity to 18,660 million gallons. The total cost of the dam was £476,948.

Unique in its day, the Haweswater dam is a hollow concrete buttress type of dam. It makes use of the immense compressive strength of concrete and was cheaper to build and is easier to maintain than the more traditional solid gravity dam. It can be inspected and maintained from within. Possible movement of the dam is monitored by a massive plumb bob hanging inside to indicate the vertical. This marker deflected one twentieth of an inch from the vertical when the dam first filled to overflowing in 1942.

Since that time Manchester's thirst for Lake District water has not abated, but the developments at Ullswater and Windermere have reflected the immense public concern to protect the National Park. Ullswater and Windermere pumping stations are underground, soundproofed and completely hidden. Both stations are remotely operated from the treatment works at Watchgate, north of Kendal. The Ullswater station, near Pooley Bridge, pumps water up the fellside to Tarn Moor tunnel from where it flows to Heltondale and on to Haweswater. The Windermere station pumps water to a balancing reservoir at Banner Rigg from where it flows to Watchgate.

Mardale Green and the Dun bull in 1820

Martindale Old Church
and the avaricious Richard Birkett

Written records show that the old church of Martindale dates back to at least 1541. The ancient yew tree in the churchyard, now known to be 1300 years old, indicates that there has been a church on this site for a very long time.

Martindale Old Church

Although not used for regular services since 1881 the church is well kept and open to view. The pulpit bears the date 1634 and the flagged floor was laid in 1714 to replace the earthen floor.

The font is believed to have been a roman altar brought down from the Roman road of High Street about 500 years ago. It was originally used as a holy water stoup and later as the font. The deep scratches on the side of the font were made many centuries ago in the sharpening of tools.

Clarke, in his Survey of the Lakes (1789), remarks on the smallness of the stipend paid to the curate at Martindale in days gone by. In spite of this Mr Richard Birkett, who served the curacy for sixty seven years, amassed a considerable fortune. When he took up the post he was said to possess only two shirts and one suit of clothes. The 'living' consisted of of an endowment of Ł2 15s. 4d. per annum (Ł2.77 a year or 5p a week). A small house was provided and about four acres of land. Being the only person except one in the parish who could write, he transacted all the legal affairs of his 200 parishioners. Whenever he lent money he deducted, at the time of lending, interest at two shillings in the pound and the term of the loan never exceeded a year. Whenever he wrote a receipt he charged two pence and for a promissary note, fourpence and 'used such other acts of extortion as one would scarce believe to have been practised in so contracted a sphere' (Clarke's words). He also served as parish clerk and was the local schoolmaster. In addition to his school fees he had a fortnight's free board and lodging at the house of each of his scholars and at Easter was paid in eggs. These he collected himself, carrying with him a board with a hole in

Martindale Old Church

it to serve as a gauge and *'he politely refused to accept any which would pass through'*. Although the living was only worth seventeen pounds a year, through his enterprise, economies, and the exploitation of his parishioners, the Reverend Birkett was able to leave his wife twelve hundred pounds when he died.

This custom of taking board and lodging from parishioners was common in former times, as church livings were so poor, and was known as 'Whittle Gate.' *Whittle* (or knife) and *Gate* (free board) at every farm or other house in the parish, turn and turn about for a week together. The parson also took casual employment, sheep shearing, hay making, teaching etc..

Martindale Old Church can be visited. It is situated in Martindale; a beautiful remote valley down the east side of Ullswater. Drive from Pooley Bridge to Howtown and then over the Hause, past Martindale New Church and take the road which bears left to Christy Bridge. Martindale Old Church is on the left just before the bridge.

The Nab lies at the head of Martindale.It forms part of the Martindale Deer Forest and has been the home of a herd of red deer for hundreds of years.

Looking down Martindale to the Nab

Transport on Ullswater long ago

There is a comfortable inn at Pooley Bridge, on the foot of Ullswater, and another at Patterdale, a little distance from it's head. They both furnish boats upon the lake, and the long wanted medium of land conveyance is now in part supplied.

Horses and jaunting cars can be had at Pooley Bridge, and a post chaise and horses at Patterdale.

Jonathan Otley - The English Lakes and Adjacent Mountains - **1834**

The Name of Ullswater

The Name is possibly due to the fact that the lake is situated among mountains **'hul'** in Saxon signified a mountain. However, it is more likely that the name came from the Celtic **'Ulle'**, meaning the bend or elbow.

The Yellow Earl

Below the Nab is a large red-roofed building called 'The Bungalow'. This was the shooting lodge of the famous 'Yellow Earl' of Lonsdale (Hugh Lowther) whose rather eccentric behaviour and capacity for spending money

on sponsorship of good causes and on sport, made him a popular figure with the public at large, if not with the rest of the aristocracy. His interest in and sponsorship of boxing through The Sporting Club led to the creation of the famous 'Lonsdale Belt', the most desired prize in British boxing.

'The Bungalow' in Martindale

Hugh Lowther's lifelong liking for the colour yellow, which led to his nickname, was reflected in the livery of his large collection of carriages and later automobiles. He was the first president of the Automobile Association and reputedly allowed them to use his livery on all of their vehicles. The Yellow Earl entertained the Kaiser (The German Emperor) at Lowther Castle and at 'The Bungalow' in 1895 and again in 1902. The pomp and ceremony associated with the visits was apparently a sight to be seen. No expense was spared and Penrith was bedecked with bunting and decorations. The Kaiser arrived at Penrith railway station in the Earl's private, yellow liveried train. Thousands of people converged on the town to cheer and to watch the extensive procession of troops and carriages from Penrith to Lowther Castle.

Apparently Lord Lowther believed in giving his guests good sport. He had heard that The Kaiser was partial to shooting rabbits and so arranged for his keepers to net as many rabbits as possible and hold them concealed in the wood where they were to shoot. As he approached the wood with the German emperor he is reported to have observed " We often find a rabbit or two in here" (or words to that effect). With that he gave orders for the dogs to be sent into the wood, whereupon his keepers released the captured rabbits. In a very short time rabbits were pouring out of the wood in their hundreds, rushing past the startled Kaiser, who was shooting away at them as fast as he could. This sort of prank was typical of The Yellow Earl.

Hugh Lowther died in 1944, in his 87th year.

In recent years 'The Bungalow' has been advertised for weekly let in a holiday catalogue as a large holiday residence. One of its stated attractions is the original Victorian decor and plumbing with large iron baths etc..

Hartsop Hamlet
The Slate Quarries and the Mines

The earliest record of the name Hartsop was in a document dated 1245. The name means 'the hill of the red deer' and deer still roam wild on the hills above the village. Although now a sleepy hamlet, Hartsop long ago had a bigger population than Patterdale or Glenridding. With two mines in the area and large slate quarries on the side of Caudale Moor and Place Fell, Hartsop must have been buzzing with industry. The green slates were sledged down to Kirkstone Foot, brought on horseback to the head of the lake and then ferried down to Pooley Bridge in boats carrying between six and eight tons. The sledging of slates down the mountainside was a skilled and rather dangerous task. This was described as follows in Clarke's 'Survey of the Lakes' published in 1789.

A trailbarrow in use in more modern times (at Honister)

'A man will carry eight hundredweight at a time and go faster with it than without it: trials of that kind having been often made. The slate is laid upon a barrow, which is called a trail barrow; it has two inclining handles or stangs, between which the man is placed, going like a horse before the weight, and has nothing more to do than keep it in its tract, and prevent it from running too fast. Those who are dexterous will not sometimes set a foot on the ground for ten or twelve yards together; but the barrow will often run away with an unskilful person, which was my case when I made an attempt. The length that is so carried is here about half a mile; the ascent so steep that to many persons it is easier than the descent.'

The remains of Low Hartsop lead mine are still visible. Half a mile east of Hartsop the path towards Hayeswater crosses over Hayeswater Gill, which bears right at this point to join Pasture Beck, flowing out of Threshthwaite Cove. At the confluence of the two becks are the ruins of Low Hartsop Mine which has not been worked since 1878. A thirty foot water wheel was erected to drain the mine which suffered badly from flooding. The stone piers which you can see are the remains of the watercourse supports, and beyond is the wheelpit, with a tree growing out of it. Due to continued problems with flooding, most of the work after 1870 was carried out in the levels high on the Dodd, which can be seen from Hartsop village.

The Kirkstone Pass and Inn

The name Kirkstone (church stone) refers to the church-like rock standing at the head of the pass overlooking Brotherswater below. It was Wordsworth no less who immortalised this rock with the words:

'This block-and yon, whose church-like frame
gives to this savage pass its name.'

The Kirkstone Pass Coaching Inn dates back to the 15th century. It was built in 1496 by a priest from the Troutbeck valley, - *'in order for workers and travellers alike to stop and rest away from the harsh weather which comes without warning.'*

High on Caudale Moor, above The Kirkstone Inn is a memorial cairn. The cairn, complete with cross, is situated a couple of hundred yards to the west of the footpath from Kirkstone top to Stony Cove Pike and about half a mile from the summit of the pike.

The Kirkstone

The cairn commemorates one Mark Atkinson of Kirkstone Pass Inn who died in 1930 aged 60 and, more recently, to his son Mark Ian Atkinson who was born at the inn and died in 1987 aged 83 years.

15

The Ullswater Navigation and Transport Company

The Raven at Glenridding Pier

For over one hundred years two nineteenth century steam yachts have provided a regular service on the lake. 'The Lady of the Lake,' the smaller of the two vessels, was launched in 1877 followed by 'The Raven' in July 1889.

The Raven, built at Rutherglen near Glasgow by Joseph Seath and Company, was carried in sections by rail to Penrith and then by horse dray to Pooley Bridge, where she was assembled. During the 1930's both vessels were converted to oil burning.

A famous passenger on the Raven in 1902 was the German Kaiser, who was a guest of the famous Yellow Earl; Lord Lonsdale of Lowther Castle.

The company provide a scheduled daily service from early Spring to late Autumn between Pooley Bridge, Howtown and Glenridding. In addition, one hour cruises, cruise and lunch and special charters are available.

Echoes of Ullswater

A visitor attraction of the eighteenth century at Ullswater was to 'try the echoes.' Vessels on the lake were armed with swivel guns and on a still evening, it was said, twenty five distant reverberations could be heard from the discharge of a swivel with only two ounces of powder. Mr Hutchinson in his 'Excursion to the Lakes,' page 65, gives the following description of such an event having landed on the shores of a bay opposite Watermillock. "Whilst we sat to regale, the barge put off from shore to a station where the finest echoes were to be obtained from the surrounding mountains. The vessel was provided with six brass cannon, mounted on swivels. On discharging one of these pieces, the report was echoed from the opposite rocks, where, by reverberation, it seemed to roll from cliff to cliff, and return through every cave and valley, till the decreasing tumult gradually died away upon the ear." The practice was continued in more recent times. Behind the Patterdale Hotel is a crag known at one time as Nell Crag. In the eighteen thirties a cannon was occasionally fired from here to the great delight of the visitors.

Greenside Lead Mine
Accidents

In its long life Greenside Mine only suffered two major accidents, both occurring towards the end of the mine's life. The first of these was due to a fire which started in the north shaft over the weekend causing carbon monoxide to diffuse into the workings. On Monday 7th July 1952 a group of miners were driven back by strong fumes as they approached the lift shaft, but not before hearing the shouts of miner Leo Mulyran, who had already descended to the bottom of the shaft. In the subsequent attempt to rescue him three men died, as did Mulyran himself. The heroic rescue attempt was recognised by justly deserved medals and commendations. The second fatal accident occurred in 1960 when the mine was about to close. The Atomic Energy Authority arranged to explode two charges of TNT, one of 500 lbs and the other of 250 lbs, in order to conduct seismic tests. The data was needed to calibrate instruments which would be used to monitor underground nuclear explosions. The charges were fired electrically from the surface but only the larger one went off. After the explosion the mine was ventilated and declared safe but two men, who later went in, were asphyxiated by an isolated pocket of gas trapped in one of the stopes. At the time the secrecy surrounding the project, and the involvement of the Atomic Energy Authority, led to rumours that a small atomic bomb had been exploded in the mine.

Greenside Mine

17

Keppel Cove Dam Flood

At 1.30 a.m. on Saturday, 29th October 1927, after a period of exceptional rainfall, the earthen wall of Keppel Cove Tarn Dam burst, causing a great wall of water to descend on Glenridding far below. The size of the deluge was such that it left a gap in the dam 80ft wide by 60ft deep. The flood rushed down Glenridding Beck carrying away Rattle Beck bridge, flooding houses alongside the beck and Eagle Farm to a depth of five to six feet. Debris, including dead sheep and a tea hut, was deposited on the other side of the lake near Side Farm. The basement bedrooms of the Glenridding Hotel were flooded and four sleeping girls floated up to the ceiling on their mattresses. One of these had a near escape as she was swept through a window but was then saved by one Ernest Thompson. The peninsula at Glenridding, which is now the site of the steamer pier, was formed as a result of this flood which also brought down a mass of large rocks with it. The rocks were used to build up this strip of land which is now a popular recreation area for visitors. The Keppel Cove earth dam was replaced by a rough concrete dam which also burst, but less spectacularly, in 1931. The second dam is still to be seen complete with large hole in the base.

The remains of the concrete dam at Keppelcove

Charles Gough

An unfortunate early hillwalker

The large stone memorial, which stands on the summit plateau of Helvellyn directly above Red Tarn, records an event that has since become famous through the attentions of the Lakeland poets. The carved stone, set into a cairn, records the death of Charles Gough of Manchester who perished in the spring of 1805 when attempting to cross from Patterdale to Wythburn. A fall of snow had partially obscured the path and he apparently fell from the head of Red Cove onto the rocks below. His dog, which accompanied him on

Charles' Gough Memorial

that fateful day, remained with the body until it was found three months later by William Harrison of Hartsop. It was this act of extreme devotion which captured the imagination of both Wordsworth and Scott. Scott's verses on 'Helvellyn' refer to the event and Wordsworth's 'Fidelity' tells the tale in full (see the section on Wordsworth).

Charles Gough's remains are buried at Tirril between Pooley Bridge and Penrith. There is speculation how the dog, a terrier bitch named Foxey, survived for three months on the mountain.

Some say the dog fed on rabbits, or sheep, or stray birds. But one thing is certain, the flesh on the man's legs was completely eaten and nothing left but the bones. Canon Rawnsley in his book 'Literary Associations of the English Lakes' disputes the suggestion that Foxey ate the remains of her master. He quotes a letter dated Yanwath 30th of Eighth month 1805 which contains a brief note of the incident. In that letter, written only six months after the event, it is stated that: 'his bones were bleached white though covered with his clothes, and his skull was separated and found at a distance from the rest. --- His faithful dog had attended his relics between three and four months, but how it had subsisted itself is difficult to suppose, though it appeared to the people who collected his remains that it eat grass' Foxey gave birth to pups during her vigil which were found dead. Further evidence says Rawnsley that Foxey survived only

Charles Gough

on grass and carrion mutton which did not provide enough sustenance to support her pups. This controversy arose as a result of a mischievous tale written by the minor poet Christopher North (Professor Wilson), who suggested that *'The Red Tarn Club'* of Ravens set to work on Gough's remains.

Canon Rawnsley was a prime mover in having the memorial stone erected. The front cover of this book depicts an early photograph from Rawnsley's book 'Gough and his Dog'. The photograph is dated June 18th 1891 and shows Gough's memorial being erected on the summit of Helvellyn. Canon Rawnsley is the bearded gentlemen standing second from the left. The stone carries verses from Wordsworth's poem 'Fidelity' and Rawnsley's initials HDR can be seen inscribed at the bottom righthand corner. It must have

Building the Cairn to Charles Gough on Helvellyn (1891)

been quite a journey up for the horse in the picture, which presumably pulled the stone up on a sled from Patterdale via the Grisedale pack horse path and then onto Dollywaggon Pike and hence to the summit.

Charles Gough was an early tourist victim of the fells although, from what we know, he was by no means an inexperienced walker in these hills, which he visited often. The fact that he is so well known and has had a monument raised to his memory has more to do with the faithfulness of his dog, Foxey and the fact that this extreme act of devotion caught the imagination of the Lake Poets, particularly Wordsworth and Scott.

Charles Gough

A letter from Charles to his older brother, Harry, survives in the British Library, which gives an insight into his character, lifestyle and associates, as well as a description of an earlier ascent of the mountain which was to claim his life a few months later. Charles Gough was born in Manchester on 18th April 1782 of Quaker parents. He often visited his brother who lived at Crosby Garrett near Kirby Stephen. The letter was written to his brother not long after he had stayed with him. In the letter Gough describes the part of his journey between Skipton and Grasmere after leaving his brother's home. It illustrates very well the difficulties in moving around the countryside in those days, compared to today.

Gough set off from Skipton about 10 a.m., making his way towards Stavely (a distance of some forty eight miles) in 'not very heavy rain' and arriving very wet at about 2 p.m.. Here he lunched and, observing an Ambleside Chaise on its way to Kendal, decided to wait for it's return, during which time he dried out his clothes.

He caught the Chaise, four hours later, arriving in Ambleside at about 8 p.m.. Here he 'had the good fortune to meet there with the Keswick Chaise just going off with three ladies'. He obtained a seat with them and arrived at Grasmere about 9 p.m., having travelled a total distance of about 56 miles in 11 hours, an average of about 5 miles per hour. Today, of course, the same journey would take about one hour.

View from the summit of Helvellyn

Gough goes on to describe how he set out to climb Helvellyn at 2 p.m. on November 6th 1804; a mild day. He must have been quite fit as he arrived at the summit in only one and a half hours, from where he described the view: *The distant view was not so clear as I have been used to see it - so that I have not opportunity of observing whether the mountain which I suspect to be Wild Boar Fell, is so or not. I could not even discern it. Cross Fell was quite misty as were all the mountains to the NE & N so much so that I could not see the Beacon upon Penrith Fell - tho' I could see the town very fair. Skiddaw and Saddleback appeared as well as ever I saw them, so*

Charles Gough

did most of the great mountains in Borrowdale and Buttermere. Ullswater &
Bassenthwaite water to N & NE were clear. Winandermere, Esthwaite & Coniston
waters were not to say very clear. the (sic.) Bay of Morecambe I could barely
distinguish, and the Sea off Whitehaven & Maryport I could not see at all, nor
Solway Frith - how ever I was well satisfied with my excursion. the top of Helvellyn
is covered with a light Snow which fell on Saturday evening. Skiddaw had also
some Snow on its Summit on Sunday but I saw no remain of it to Day. At 25
minutes past 4 I began to descend and reached the bottom at 5 precisely (pretty
quick again) I am now writing at the foot of this immense mountain, where I have
been since Saturday when I left Grassmere for a few days.'

Sadly, on his return to Helvellyn during the following February, Gough was
to lose his life in circumstances which would lead to his story being
remembered and told nearly two hundred years later.

Helvellyn's other memorials

There are two other memorials on Helvellyn. A white painted iron plaque
marks the spot where Robert Dixon of Rookings, Patterdale, died on 27th
May 1858, while following the Patterdale Foxhounds.

The third memorial is to be found a hundred yards or so south of the
summit shelter beside the path leading towards Wythburn. A recently
re-erected plaque records the first landing of an aircraft on the summit of
an English mountain. On the 22nd December 1926, pilots John Leeming
and Bert Hinkler landed an Avro 585 Gosport aeroplane on the summit
plateau. After a short stay they then flew back to Woodford in Cheshire.
(Woodford is very near the present Manchester Airport).

Bad weather in Patterdale

If it is very windy in Patterdale and you are walking on Place Fell (the fell to
the east of the village), then perhaps you should wear a safety helmet. Mrs
Little records in 'The Chronicles of Patterdale' (Women's Institute) how, on
one very windy day in 1951, a corrugated iron garage belonging to the
White Lion Hotel in Patterdale was blown to bits and pieces of the
corrugated iron were scattered in and around the village. One piece soared
higher than the rest and came down on Boredale Hause, half way up Place
Fell, having travelled a distance of about half a mile and achieved a vertical
ascent of at least eight hundred feet.

King of Patterdale

Among the cottages of this village (Patterdale) there is a house belonging to a person of somewhat better condition; whose little estate, which he occupies himself, lies in the neighbourhood. As his property, inconsiderable as it is, is better than that of any of his neighbours, it has given him the title of *King of Patterdale,* in which his family name is lost. His ancestors have long enjoyed the title before him. We had the honour of seeing this prince and he took the diversion of fishing on the lake; and I could not help thinking, that if I were inclined to envy the situation of any potentate in Europe, it would be that of the King of Patterdale. The pride of Windsor and Versailles would shrink in comparison with the magnificence of his dominions. **William Gilpin ‑1772**

Gilpin was referring to the Mounsey family who lived at Patterdale Hall for many generations, flourishing and spreading to many neighbouring villages. According to tradition it was a Mounsey who led the statesmen of Patterdale to victory, when, in the narrow passage of the road between Ullswater and the hill above, just where the boundary line between Cumberland and Westmorland used to run, they defeated a stong group of Scottish Raiders, who had come to plunder their peaceful valley. From then on the Mounsey's were known as The Kings of Patterdale.

James Clarke in his "Survey of the Lakes" quotes an amusing anecdote about Mr John Mounsey, last but one of the Kings of Patterdale. Mr Mounsey had a few goats upon the neighbouring mountains which were extremely wild and so difficult to take that, having sold four to a butcher for two guineas, the butcher paid no less than thirty shillings for catching them, and the takers even had reason to complain of their bargain.

Clarke goes on to relate how on one occasion Mr Mounsey made him a

Lakeland Goat

present of some kids, upon the condition that he should catch them for himself. He set out to do so next day with eleven men and dogs, but found the pursuit a most difficult one. At last they cornered a goat in a craggy position near "Eusey" (Aira) Force, from which there seemed to be no escape, but the goat charged the dog, who was attacking him, and fell with him over the precipice. The goat got up after the fall and got away, but the dog was killed.

Next day ten men set out on a second expedition, but brought home only one kid.

23

The Story of 'The Parting Stone'

An ancient packhorse route wends its way between Patterdale and Grasmere, climbing up the Grisedale Pass to Grisedale Tarn, before descending into Grasmere. At the head of the pass, a short distance east of the tarn stands a large stone with an iron notice fixed in it carrying the words 'The Parting Stone'. Closer examination of the stone reveals an inscription carved in the rock carrying verses from William Wordsworth's Elegiac Verses " In memory of my brother John Wordsworth."

This is a lament at the loss of his brother John in a shipwreck. John was master of The East Indiaman 'The Earl of Abergavenny'. During his leave from sea he often stayed with William and Dorothy at Dove Cottage. When the time came for John to return to his ship, he would take the track from Grasmere, via Grisedale Tarn, over to Patterdale. From there he would take a coach to Penrith. William always set John upon his way by accompanying him as far as the top of Grisedale where, at a large stone, he would bid his brother farewell and watch him as he descended down into Patterdale.

Shortly after one of these farewells, on the night of Friday, February 5th 1805, John's ship was wrecked on The Shambles, off the Portland Bill, through the incompetence of the pilot. William recorded this sad happening in a poem of lament, which he composed at the *parting stone*. A short excerpt is given on the next page:

The Parting Stone

'The Parting Stone'

I

The sheep boy whistled loud and lo!
That instant, startled by the shock,
The buzzard mounted from the rock
Deliberate and slow:
Lord of the air, he took his flight:
Oh! could he on that woeful night
Have lent his wing, my brother dear,
For one poor moment's space to thee
And all who struggled with the sea
When safety was so near.

III

Here did we stop and here look round,
While each into himself descends,
For that last thought of parting friends
That is not to be found.......

Queen of the Mountains

Helvellyn and her companions while not exactly within the inner sanctum
are yet not subsidiary to Scafell. If Scafell is thought of as the King of the
Lake mountains, then Helvellyn is more like the Queen than the Prince.
(Perhaps burly Skiddaw, the only other peak to over - top 3,000 ft. is the
Prince). She is of equal importance with King Scafell in the general scheme
and below her spreads like a train the beautiful lake of Ullswater. She is more
accessible, too, as a Queen should be, than Scafell, and on her Striding edge,
that famous dizzy walk, she offers the adventurous tourist the slightly spurious
thrill of a danger that looks greater than it is ....

E.F. Bozman, The English Countryside

A serious young lady from Welwyn
took a cookery book up Helvellyn.
while reading the recipes
She fell down a precipice,
And that was the end of poor Ellen

Lakeland Limericks   **Gibbs 1942**

King Dunmail

and the Battle of Dunmail Raise

The story of King Dunmail and his last battle at Dunmail Raise in the year 945 is steeped in Arthurean legend. There are several versions of the story, some more fanciful than others. The description here is a compilation of these.

Dunmail was the son of Owain, one of the strongest of the Cumbrian kings who came to the throne about 920. Owain is generally thought to have been Sir Gawain, one of the principal characters of Arthurian legend, however the dates don't really match up. Owain was descended from the old Caesarian line of the kings of Strathclyde, who by this time had lost much of their power and influence due to attacks from Anglian invaders, who encroached

Dunmail's Cairn

into the Scottish lowlands. Owain ruled his kingdom from Penrith, as Carlisle had been sacked by the Danes in 876 and was a ruin. Indeed Carlisle remained virtually abandoned for almost 200 years. The seven tombs forming the 'Giant's Grave' and the 'Giant's Thumb' in Penrith churchyard date back to this time and indicate that Penrith was an important centre. The popular tradition which says that the monuments are the tomb of a giant, 'Hugh or Owen Caesarius,' probably records some dim memory of Owain. Owain, together with his uncle, King Constantine II of the Scots, plotted with the Vikings of Galloway and the Isles against the English King Athelstan, to whom they had previously sworn allegiance as King of all Britain. This led to a great battle in the year 938 on the flat topped mountain near Ecclefechan in Galloway, called Burnswark, at which the English were victorious. What happened to Owain after the battle is not recorded, but Dunmail, his son and successor, apparently did not learn from this experience. Dunmail continued his dangerous alliance with the Vikings of Galloway and the Isles.

26

King Dunmail

King Edmund, the Saxon king, who succeeded Athelstan on the English throne, was quick to act, sending an army across Stainmore which defeated Dunmail at a place unknown. After this battle, Edmund, with the usual barbarity of the times, put out the eyes of Dunmail's two sons and gave his country to Malcolm; King of Scotland, on condition he preserved peace in the northern parts of England. Although several sites for the battle have been suggested, including Orrest Head at Windermere, legend and popular belief portray Dunmail Raise as the battleground. The story of the battle is interwoven with legend and superstition but is a fine tale to hear. I quote from an account given in 1927 in 'Cycling' magazine by one W.T. Palmer.

The Raise has legend of one mighty battle a thousand years ago. King Edmund the Saxon was quelling the raider Britons on his border, and Dunmail of Cumberland came in for punitive attention. The armies met on this level among the hills, and a formless pile of stones marks the burial place of those who fell. Here is a pretty legend:

The crown of Dunmail of Cumberland was charmed, giving its wearer a succession in his kingdom. Therefore King Edmund the Saxon coveted it above all things. When Dunmail came to the throne of the mountain land a wizard in Gilsland Forest held a master charm to defeat the promise of his crown. He Dunmail slew. The magician was able to make himself invisible save at cock crow and to destroy him the hero braved a cordon of wild wolves at night. At the first peep of dawn, he entered the cave where the wizard was lying. Leaping to his feet the magician called out "Where river runs north or south with the storm," ere Dunmail's sword silenced him.

The story came to the ear of the covetous Saxon, who, after much enquiry of his priests, found that an incomplete curse, although powerful against Dunmail, could scarcely hurt another holder of the crown. Spies were accordingly sent into Cumbria to find where a battle could be fought favourable to the magician's words. On Dunmail Raise, in times of storm even in unromantic today, the torrent sets north or south in capricious fashion. The spies found the place, found also fell land chiefs who were persuaded to become secret allies of the Saxon. The campaign began.

Dunmail moved his army south to meet the invader, and they joined battle in the pass. For long hours the battle was with the Cumbrians; the Saxons were driven down the hill again and again. As his foremost tribes became exhausted, Dunmail retired and called on his reserves - they were mainly the ones favouring the southern

King Dunmail

king. On they came, spreading in well - armed lines from side to side of the hollow way, but instead of opening to let the weary warriors through, they delivered an attack on them. Surprised, the army reeled back and their rear was attacked with redoubled violence by the Saxons. The loyal ranks were forced to stand back to back round their king; assailed by superior forces they fell rapidly, and ere long the brave chief was shot down by a traitor of his own bodyguard.

"My crown," cried he, " bear it away; never let the Saxon flaunt it." A few stalwarts took the charmed treasure from his hands, and with a furious onslaught made the attackers give way. Step by step they fought their way up the ghyll of Dunmail's beck - broke through all resistance on the open fell, and, aided by a dense cloud, evaded their pursuers. Two hours later the faithful few met by Grisedale Tarn, and consigned the crown to its depths -

"till Dunmail come again to lead us." And every year the warriors come back, draw up the magic circlet from the depths of the wild mountain tarn, and carry it with them over Seat Sandal to where the king is sleeping his age long sleep. They knock with his spear on the topmost stone of the cairn and from its heart comes a voice. "Not yet; not yet - wait a while my warriors."

Grisedale Tarn in winter

Another legend says that Dunmail did not die in the battle; that he survived for thirty years in Strathclyde and died a pilgrim in Rome. Be that as it may, Edmund did not gain a successor for his throne. Four years after the battle on Dunmail Raise he was assassinated, and his kingdom went into ruin.

28

The Shepherd of Greenhead Ghyll
'Michael'

This tale, told by Wordsworth in his poem *'Michael'*, was probably based on a family that lived in Grasmere Vale. A field adjacent to Greenhead Ghyll is called 'Michael's Fold' and the site of a ruined building high above Grasmere looks out over views similar to those described in the verse. The poem is very long and so I will only relate a brief synopsis of the tale:

Long ago a shepherd called Michael was married to a wife, Isabel, twenty years his junior. They were blessed late in life with an only son called Luke. From the age of ten Luke worked with his father, who was then sixty six, day in and day out. In the evening they would rest in their cottage which was high on the side of Greenhead Ghyll and could be seen from Grasmere and the surrounding vale. Every night Isabel lit a lamp to see them home which, as it stood in the window of the cottage, could be seen by the whole valley. This light became famous and was named *'The Evening Star'* by the residents of Grasmere Vale. Unfortunately, due to the misfortune of his brother's son who failed in business, Michael, who had agreed to be bound in surety for his nephew, had to give up half of his living to cover the debt. The farm could no longer support both he and his son. Luke, who was eighteen years old at this time, had to leave and live with a relative in the city who agreed to try and find work for the lad. Before Luke left, his father and he laid the foundations of a new sheepfold beside the ghyll which, Michael promised, would be ready for his son's return, when his fortune was made. While his son

Greenhead Ghyll, Grasmere

Michael

was away Michael added to the sheepfold in his spare moments, ever looking forward to Luke's eventual return. Alas it was not to be. Luke soon became influenced by city life and turned to drink, gambling and coarse living. The old man lost heart when he heard the news and realised that Luke was not coming back. Michael finally died at the age of ninety one, with the sheepfold still unfinished. Isobel survived a further few years before the estate was sold and *'went into a stranger's hand'*.

Wordsworth relates how the cottage which was named the *'Evening Star'* has gone, a ploughshare has been through the ground on which it stood. Yet the oak is left that grew beside the door. A possible site for the cottage is immediately west of Alcock Tarn where the remains of a house built into the hillside is to be seen. A few yards further down the slope to the right of the cottage are the rotten remains of a large tree stump. The view from this point is just as the poem describes, encompassing Grasmere Vale, Easedale and Dunmail Raise. There is no sign of an unfinished sheepfold beside the Ghyll, but there are the remains of the old mine buildings of the Greenhead Ghyll. Perhaps the unfinished sheepfold was incorporated into the mine building.

The 'Lion and the Lamb'
or 'The Old Woman playing the Organ'

The intriguing rocky summit of Helm Crag above Grasmere has borne these popular names for many yeats. The summit rocks can be construed to depict either of the above depending on your viewpoint from the valley below.

The Borrowdale Cuckoo & other Tales

The folk of Cumberland and Westmorland generally used to think of the Borrowdale people as rather simple and unsophisticated. In the same way that an Englishman tells Irish jokes, or a German tells jokes about the Swiss, so the Burghers of Keswick told tales about the inhabitants of Borrowdale. Harriet Martineau related several of these in her book 'English Lakes' published in 1855.

To preserve these stories for posterity I reproduce three of them in full below:

It is said that an old Borrowdale man was once sent a very long way for something very new, by some innovator who had found his way into the dale. The man was to go with horse and sacks (for there were no carts, because there was no road) to bring some lime from beyond Keswick. On his return, when he was near Grange, it began to rain; and the man was alarmed at seeing his sacks begin to smoke. He got a hatful of water from the river; but the smoke grew worse. Assured at length that the devil must be in any fire that was aggravated by water, he tossed the whole load over into the river.

The Borrowdale Cuckoo

That must have been before the dalesmen built their curious wall; for they must have had lime for that. Spring being very charming in Borrowdale, and the sound of the cuckoo gladsome, the people determined to build a wall to keep in the cuckoo, and make the spring last forever. So they built a wall across the entrance, at Grange. The plan did not answer; but that was, according to the popular belief from generation to generation, because the wall was not built one course higher. It is simply for want of a top course in that wall that eternal spring does not reign in Borrowdale.

Another anecdote shows, however, that a bright wit did occasionally show himself among them. A "statesman" (an "estateman," or small proprietor) went one day to a distant fair or sale, and brought home what neither he nor his neighbours had ever seen before; - a pair of stirrups. Home he came jogging, with his feet in his stirrups; but, by the time he reached his own

The Borrowdale Cuckoo & other Tales

door, he had jammed his feet in so fast that they would not come out. There was great alarm and lamentation; but, as it could not be helped now, the good man patiently sat his horse in the pasture for a day or two, his family bringing him food, till the eldest son, vexed to see the horse suffering by exposure, proposed to bring both into the stable. This was done; and there sat the farmer for several days, - his food being brought to him, as before. At length, it struck the second son that it was a pity not to make his father useful, and release the horse; so he proposed to carry him, on the saddle, into the house. By immense exertion it was done; the horse being taken alongside the midden in the yard, to ease the fall: and the good man found himself under his own roof again, - spinning wool in a corner of the kitchen. There the mounted man sat spinning, through the cleverness of his second son, till the lucky hour arrived of his youngest son's return, - he being a scholar, - a learned student from St Bees. After duly considering the case, he gave his counsel. He suggested that the good man should draw his feet out of his shoes. This was done, amidst the blessings of the family; and the good man was restored to his occupations and to liberty. The wife was so delighted that she said if she had a score of children, she would make them all scholars, - if only she had to begin life again.

The Great Deed of Borrowdale

The manor of 'Barrowdale,' (Dale of the Castle), had been granted to the monks of Furness Abbey by the Derwentwater family. At the dissolution of the monasteries the property reverted to the Crown and was later sold by James I to two Londoners. For reasons unknown, these two worthies promptly sold the estate to the tenants for less than a single year's revenue and the contract for this sale, dated 1613, became known as :
'The Great Deed of Borrowdale.'

Weather Lore
The Borrowdale Sop

The Borrowdale Sop is a small cloud that rises at times at the head of Borrowdale near Piers Ghyll.

Gradually growing larger it floats away down the Derwent Valley over Styhead Tarn. If it goes over towards the vale of St John the weather will continue to be fine, but if it takes the direction of Langdale, rain will follow within the next twenty-four hours.

Millican Dalton

Hermit and Adventurer of Castle Crag, Borrowdale

Castle Crag is the site of an old British hill fort which was used by the local inhabitants for their protection. This was necessary after the departure of the Romans left them vulnerable to other invaders. West, writing in 1779, tells us that much freestone, both red and white, was quarried out of the ruins. He

Castle Crag in Borrowdale

also records that an iron bow and two masses of smelted iron were taken out of them, evidence for iron age occupation. In more recent times Castle Crag has been used as a slate quarry, as is readily evident when one climbs up and investigates.

There are ancient records of a hermit living on Castle Crag, but we know far more of the 20th century hermit; one Millican Dalton. Millican was an early refugee from the rat race of the city. He was born at Nenthead near Alston in 1867 and worked at a shipping office in London until the age of thirty. A lover of the simple life, he then gave up his job to become a professional camper and guider leading organised tours in the Lake District, Scotland and Switzerland. When in England, he divided his time between Epping Forest and the Lake District, spending three months every summer in a man-made cave on Castle Crag. He soon became quite famous being known as 'The

Millican Dalton

Professor of Adventure' and would give instruction in the art of raft building and sailing as well as rock climbing. Millican was a colourful character. He made his own clothes and equipment, wore shorts, a slouch hat with pheasant's feather, and a tweed coat. He was also a strict vegetarian and a Quaker. The picture of Millican on his raft on the Derwent was even sold to tourists as a postcard. The hermit of Castle Crag finally died in 1947 at the age of 80. One memorial to Millican still exists; one that was wrought by his own hand. At the entrance to the upper cave, his sleeping quarters known as 'The Attic,' one can still see the carving on the wall of his favourite saying:

(To get the intended meaning put an 'or' between Worrds and Jump).

Mabel M Barker, a longtime friend of Millican, wrote an obituary to him shortly after his death in 1947, which gives an interesting insight into his lifestyle and character. In it she describes how he left his office job to live on a tiny income on a piece of land in Billericay, Essex. Later he deserted even that to live in a tent on a small flat space above High Lodore Farm during the Summer. In the winter he resided in a hut in Epping Forest. He augmented the little income he had by 'making tents and rucksacks, and by initiation of budding mountaineers'.

She first met Millican in 1913 when she hired tents from him for a party of students to camp at Seathwaite. He reminded her of Robinson Crusoe. I quote: 'He made his own clothes, very strong and efficient, entirely of his own design and of a dull green, toning with the fells. But whether from choice or a streak of laziness (I do not think I ever saw him in a hurry) they were never quite finished, the edges remaining unhemmed. A red plaid added colour, and was put to innumerable uses. A slouch hat always bore a pheasant's feather. Bright blue eyes sparkled in a permanently tanned face, and a little pointed beard was slightly grey even then.' (Millican would be 46 in 1913). Mabel Barker goes on to explain how he introduced her to climbing and how careful and patient he was with

Millican Dalton

novices, never putting them at risk or taking them beyond their ability. '*He really taught his initiates, explaining and showing the use of belays, knots (I was never really happy in the use of any knots but his), the safe length of a pitch, care for the leader and the general safety of the whole party.*' Millican never charged for his services, except for small camping expenses. He climbed until he was 80, not only in this country but abroad. In 1922, Millican led a party (including Mabel) to Mayerhofen in the Austrian Tyrol. Here Dalton '*dealt patiently with a company ranging from middle-aged women to small boys, and taught many of us all we ever learned about negotiating the glaciers and snowfields.*' Soon after this Millican gave up the campsite at High Lodore and moved into the cave on Castle Crag. '*There he was to be found, summer after summer, and we could tell when he was at home by the blue smoke curling among the trees, easily seen from the Borrowdale Road.*' In spite of his lifestyle Millican was not one for 'roughing it'. He was adept at achieving comfort wherever possible. He believed in down quilts when camping and wore a large square of Willesden canvas on the seat of his breeches, thus ensuring that his waterproof groundsheet went with him.

Millican Dalton on his raft on the Derwent

Mabel Barker concludes with the observation that '*He had , I think, early worked out a theory of life for himself, and if ever anyone did so, he lived up to it consistently and completely. He had found something, and was well content with it. Into this union and practice of life, climbing fitted as a natural part. He did things on the rocks, as everywhere else, to please himself, but not for self-seeking; to fit in with his theory of life, and of earth and his relation to it.*'

Millican Dalton's cave on the eastern slopes of Castle Crag can be visited. Take the path from Grange village which leads south to the campsite in Dalt Wood, beside the river. Follow the path by the riverside which crosses a stream (Broadslack Gill) into Low Hows Wood (NT). Take the path which leads south through the middle of the wood and look for evidence of old quarry workings to your right as you pass under Castle Crag. The cave is among these workings at grid reference NY253 159 (O.S. 1:25000 map North West sheet).

The carving mentioned above is to be found at the entrance to the upper cave '*The Attic*'.

Mining in the Derwent Fells

Goldscope, the German Miners, the Keswick Smelter

Mining of gold, silver, copper and lead in the Derwent Fells is known to have taken place as early as the 13th century. However large scale working of the mine under Hindscarth, in the Newlands valley, commenced with the arrival of the German Miners in 1564.

Goldscope Mine, on the lower slopes of Hindscarth

Queen Elizabeth the first is reputed to have desired that England should have its own supplies of copper, a strategic metal in time of war, as it was used for 'copperbottoming' her warships. This process prevented the formation of barnacles on the wooden hulls and ensured maximum speed for the fleet.

The Germans were acknowledged to be the most skilled deep miners in the world and so, in 1568, 'The Mines Royal' company was set up to exploit the mineral reserves of the Lake District. Miners from Augsburg under the direction of one Daniel Hechstetter commenced operations at Goldscope. They worked the mine for copper and obviously found it profitable as they called the mine 'Gottesgab' or God's Gift. Over the years this has become distorted to the present 'Goldscope.' The Germans were not well received by the locals, who were jealous of their prosperity and ability to attract the local girls. They were frequently attacked and occasionally murdered. Eventually, however, they became integrated into the community, as can be seen from the names on some of the gravestones in the grounds of Newlands church. Indeed many well known surnames in the county such as the Tullies of

36

Goldscope Mine

Carlisle, the Banks of Keswick, the Nicholson's of Hawkshead Hall, and the Rawlinson's of Grisedale originated in these early unions between the German miners and local families. Other names, still to be found in the phone book, are Senogles and Stamper (Stampfer).

Thomas Percy, Earl of Northumberland, on whose property Goldscope and several other mines lay, was also ill disposed to the mining activities. He received no benefit from the operations of the 'Mines Royal Company' and obstructed their activities whenever possible. His conflict with the Crown led to litigation and eventually armed rebellion. As a prominent catholic he was goaded into this rebellion by the Queen, who demanded, through her company, retrospective royalties and fines for the years that he had worked the mines, before the advent of the 'Mines Royal Company'. Elizabeth made the absurd claim that the metal extracted from the mines was hers, because the gold extracted from the ores was worth more than the lead and copper

The Borrowdale mineral spring

One piece of real estate mentioned in the Great Deed of Borrowdale (see page 32) was a saline spring with medicinal properties, which had been discovered and used by the early German miners. The Salt Well, as it became known, was once very popular and featured in Thomas Short's 'History of Mineral Waters', published in 1740. Visitors who came to sample the waters would stay at Manesty House; which is situated near the well. Salt water is also to be found in an old mineshaft in the field adjacent to the well.

Borrowdale Salt Well today (recently restored), with Manesty House in the background

Goldscope Mine, the Keswick Smelter

combined. It was this typical act of Tudor injustice which led to the rebellion and Lord Percy's eventual downfall, along with many other northern catholic families. He was finally executed for insurrection and his head was displayed on one of the gates of York.

Mining continued at Goldscope and other mines in the area, without much success, until about 1650. The ore from the mines was smelted at the Keswick Smelter, situated on Lord's Island, Derwentwater. Fuel for the smelter came from Newlands and from Wythop Woods, on the western shore of Bassenthwaite. The effect on the landscape was drastic as the woods were cut

Mediaeval Oak Forest in Newlands

down. The small clumps of stunted trees which can still be seen high on the southern slopes of Causey Pike are the remnants of the original mediaeval forest in Newlands, that covered the valley prior to 1560. Unfortunately the advent of the Civil War brought death and destruction to the area. Cromwell's army destroyed the smelter and most of the miners were either killed or drafted into the army. For about thirty years the mines were abandoned until, in about 1690, a band of Dutchmen, who came over with William of Orange, re- opened them. The mining of copper at Goldscope eventually petered out with the development of Coniston as a copper mining centre. For the first half of the nineteenth century lead was mined, with little success, under a number of different owners. Then, in 1849, it was purchased by a private company of four men named Clarke, Chapman, Horne and Hart. Initially they had little success and by 1850 the mine was in debt to the amount of L3726 7s 4d. Mr Hart became unable to pay his quota of the expenses and forfeited his shares, Mr Horn retired and, not long after, Mr Chapman relinquished his shares and sailed for Australia.

This left Mr Clarke to soldier on alone and his perseverance was rewarded when the great lead vein was discovered and the mine really did become God's gift. In a twelve year period, about 5000 tons of lead ore was raised,

Goldscope Mine

which also yielded 22000 ozs of silver. The mine continued to return a substantial profit until 1864 when production had to cease. The mine had been driven so deep that the 40 ft waterwheel, used to drain it, could no longer do its work. It was considered to be too risky a venture to invest money on new machinery, so the mine closed.

Origins of Keswick

The name **Kesewic** first appears in writing in a document about 1234 relating to the purchase of land by William de Derwentwater from the monks of the Furness Abbey. Part of the deal gave the monks *'leave to have a mill dam on William's land of Kesewic'*.

This is simply *'Kese wic'* or the cheese dairy of the Derwentwater Estate. So Keswick originated from a cheese farm near Crosthwaite.

Newlands

The name Newlands derives from the draining of a tarn, 'Husaker Tarn', by the monks of Furness.
Prior to this time the valley was a rather barren and swampy place.

The monks thus reclaimed the land for cultivation, which became known as the *'new lands'*.

The name of the tarn survives to this day in the name of *'Uzzicar'* Farm, near Stair.

Lakeland Weather

Much of the rich verdant beauty of the Lake District is derived from its frequent rains; but inexperienced tourists complain bitterly of them.
For the guidance of strangers, it may be mentioned that, generally speaking, the worst months of the year, in the region, are November and December for storms; March for gales; and July for summer rains.
The driest season is usually for a month or more onwards from the middle of May. September and October are often very fine months indeed.

Harriet Martineau Guide to the Lakes published in 1855

The Ghost Army of Souther Fell

Stories of ghosts and unexplained visions are plentiful when one delves into local history. Few, however, are so well corroborated with dates, times and named observers as the story of the spectre army seen on Souther Fell. There are several versions of this happening in the eighteenth century. One of the most detailed is that of Harriet Martineau in her 'Guide to the English Lakes' of 1855.

I quote from her account :

"On Midsummer eve 1735 a farm servant in the employ of William Lancaster of Blake Hills Farm, half a mile east of Souther Fell, saw the east side of the mountain, near the summit, covered with troops, which pursued their onward march for over an hour. They came, in distinct bodies, from an eminence in the north end, and disappeared in a niche in the summit. When the poor fellow told his tale he was insulted on all hands; as original observers usually are when they see anything wonderful. Two years after, also on Midsummer's eve, Mr Lancaster saw some men there, apparently following their horses, as if they had returned from hunting. He thought nothing of this; but he happened to look up again ten minutes after, and saw the figures now mounted, and followed by an interminable array of troops, five abreast, marching from the eminence and over the cleft, as before. All the family saw this, and the manouevres of the force, as each company was kept in order by a mounted officer who galloped this way and that. As the shades of twilight came on, the discipline appeared to relax, and the troops intermingled, and rode at unequal paces, 'til all was lost in darkness. Now, of course, all the Lancasters were insulted, as their servant had been: but their justification was not long delayed. On the Midsummer day of the fearful 1745, twenty six persons, expressly summoned by the family, saw all that had been seen before and more. Carriages were now interspersed with the troops; and everybody knew that no carriages ever had been, or could be, on the summit of Souther Fell. The multitude was beyond imagination; for the troops filled a space of half a mile, and marched quickly 'til night hid them, - still marching.' There was nothing vaporous or indistinct about these spectres. So real did they seem that some of the people went up, the next morning, to look for the hoof-marks of the horses; and awful it was to them to find not one foot-print on heather or grass. The witnesses attested the whole story on oath before a magistrate; and fearful were the expectations held by the countryside about the coming events of the Scotch rebellion.

The Ghost Army of Souther Fell

It now came out that two other persons had seen something of the sort in the interval, viz., in 1743, - but had concealed it to escape the insults to which their neighbours were subjected. Mr Wren, of Wilton Hill, and his farm servant, saw, one summer evening, a man and his dog on the mountain, pursuing some horses along a place so steep that a horse could hardly, by any possibility, keep a footing on it. Their speed was prodigious, and their disappearance at the top of the fell so rapid, that Mr Wren and the servant went up, the next morning, to find the body of the man who must have been killed. Of man, horse or dog thay found not a trace: and they came down and held their tongues. When they did speak, they fared not much better for having twenty six sworn comrades in their disgrace."

So look for ghosts if you will on Souther Fell but don't expect anyone to believe you if you see them.

Blake Hills Farm with
Souther Fell behind

The Immortal Fish of Bowscale Tarn

The path up to Bowscale Tarn from the hamlet of Mosedale was a popular Victorian tourist route. Bowscale Tarn nestles in its tiny valley high on the northern side of Bowscale Fell. Its popularity was probably partly due to a folk tale dating back several centuries which tells of two immortal fish which swim in Bowscale Tarn. Wordsworth recalls the tale in his song at the feast of Brougham Castle:-

"-Both the undying fish that swim
in Bowscale Tarn did wait on him;
The pair were servants of his eye
In their immortality;
They moved about in open sight,
To and fro for his delight -"

The Crosses of Blencathra

There are two stone crosses made from large pieces of white quartz-like rock set into the ground on the plateau between the summit of Blencathra and Atkinson Pike. The larger of these was built as a labour of love over many years by Harold Robinson of Threlkeld. Harold, who died in 1988 aged 80, climbed Blencathra sometimes twice a day, each time carrying a stone for the

cross. This large white cross was built in memory of Mr Straughan, a great friend of Harold's, who was unfortunately killed while on active service in 1942. Mr Straughan in civilian life was the gamekeeper at Skiddaw House, Harold was a dedicated walker and fellrunner. According to his brother Sid, he preferred walking to using public transport. He regularly walked to Maryport and back, a distance of some forty miles. Harold's fellrunning tradition has been passed down to the present generation in the form of Kenny

Large cross on Blencathra

Stuart; the Threlkeld runner, who is related to the Robinson family. The smaller cross, which is set into the slope of the rise towards the summit of the mountain, is thought to have been built by persons unknown from stones robbed from the larger cross. It is, of course, of more recent origin than the large cross.

Skiddaw House
Originally built by Lord Lonsdale for his gamekeepers and shepherds (now a youth hostel)

Robert Pool

Evangelist and Miners Friend

Robert Pool was a rather eccentric evangelical cleric of 19th century Caldbeck. One of his main concerns was the spiritual and physical welfare of the local miners who worked in the fells around Caldbeck at that time. He recorded his observations, thoughts and poetry in a book, written in 1862, and titled: *'Thoughts on the Parish of Caldbeck.'*

This book gives a fascinating insight into life in the area at the time and dwells, in particular, on the Miners of Driggith and their lifestyle. In addition Pool, who had a great empathy with the miners, includes a poem entitled:

'The Miner's Lot'

Robert Pool explains how, in November 1859, there was a general religious awakening amongst his people. One of the public manifestations of this stir, was a daily Prayer Meeting, commenced at Driggeth Mine. As many as fourteen or more miners would meet, a few minutes before work time, at the mouth of the mine. In the words of one of the miners:

'We have no reading; we sing a hymn, such as we know, sometimes "My God, the spring of all joys." or "And am I born to die" and such like; then two engage in prayer, this is the way, and then away we go to our work.'

In his book Pool describes the local mines and how they gave employment to about one hundred miners on a regular basis, but he is very conscious of the human toll of being a mineworker in the 19th century, as shown by the following extract:

Mining is undoubtedly a very unhealthy employment, and also very laborious; the workmen ought therefore to have more than ordinary pay for extraordinary work. From the fact that this is not always the case, heart burnings arise, sometimes the fault may be the owner's, sometimes the captain's, and no doubt in some cases the blame is chargeable upon the workers themselves. But anyone watching the miner moving backward or forward to his work, will see premature old age in his looks, and in his steps, and every one thus reflecting, will say, pay him well.

Pool goes on to describe the miner's daily routine:

Picture a miner going to Roughtengill to his shift; he leaves his cot and the village before six o' clock, his slumbers were disturbed at least an hour before this; see him

Robert Pool

bending his steps towards the mountain; he has at least four miles to walk, the nearest way he can go; he often wipes the sweat from his brow, you see him to the

The path to Roughton Gill

mountain's foot, but you lose him there, he has left the balmy breeze, or the frosty winds, as the season may chance to be, to grapple with the earth's dark interior, here as he goes it is cold and chill, there it is close and foul. He pants, he toils, and sweats (he does so at least if he does his expected duty) and thus after eight hours close confinement, he again emerges into the light, to drag his weary limbs home to rest, to sleep, and again to return to his hard and dreary labour. Since this is the case, the question may be asked "are they discontented" as a class I answer for them "no," many of them can sing, and can sing heartily:

Pool then follows with the words of what can only be described as an evangelical hymn, which is obviously designed to help the miners come to terms with their harsh living conditions.

His poetry may not be of the standard of a Coleridge or a Wordsworth but it does illustrate the miner's lifestyle and eventual fate.

The Miner's Lot

In the dark winter's morn, when the winds are so bleak,
The miner goes forth, a living to seek,
The tramp of his clogs may be heard before day,
For rain, wind or snow, at home he can't stay.
He aims for the mountain with rapid stride,
He drinks at the fountain, that flows at his side;
He pants as he travels, his breathing is bad,
He sighs as he goes, his heart feels sad:
He knows that his labour will make his days less,
He would like to sojourn his children to bless,
He reaches his work, and fain would he rest,
But he strips at once, and works with zest;

44

The Miners Lot

He buckles his armour to fight for life,
He thinks of his home, his children, and wife;
He swings his pick and "smites the rock,"
The earth trembles, and owns the shock;
The glistening metal comes tumbling down,
Which is soon to be handled in the shaped half-crown:
The vapours are breathed from the sparkling earth,
Which bring to the miner premature death:
You see him look old, when he ought to look blithe,
You see him walk stiff, when he ought to walk lithe;
And what more expect, when he breathes foul air,
And has darkness and dampness alike to share.
The shepherd may think, who on the hill roams,
While the miners are sitting at ease in their homes;
The ploughman may grumble because of long hours,
And make his complaints of cold winter showers;
Let the Shepherd remember, as he wanders the hill,
That that is his lot, his duty to fill:
And the ploughman reflect on his earthly toil,
Tho the work may be hard, there is health in the soil.
The shepherd grows old, and the ploughman grows strong,
But the miner is gone to his grave ere long:
With joy let us work, in the lot we are cast,
Working and loving, to be blest at last,
With love let us try others' burdens to bear,
And meet in heaven our joys to share.
And now, as I come to the end of my song,
Let us love each other as we move along:
And as soon as we come to lay down and die,
May we all to the arms of Jesus fly.
He has made a provision that all will be blest,
He has finished a work that all may have rest.
The miner's as welcome as the queen on the throne,
All enter heaven by Jesus alone.
The rich and the poor are all alike free,
For the miner he bled and died on a tree.

Robert Pool, 1862

Sharp Edge, Blencathra
as seen by an early fellwalker

Visitors to the area in the eighteenth century often went in fear and awe of the mountains. A good example is the account following of an ascent of Sharp Edge from Scales Tarn by Mr Green; the narrator, and Mr Jonathan Otley, a well known Lakeland character of the late 18th century.

"-we crossed the stream which issues from the tarn and commenced the steep ascent at the foot of Sharp Edge. We had not gone far before we were aware that our journey would be attended with peril. The passage gradually grew narrower and the declivity on each hand awfully precipitous. From walking on it we were reduced to the necessity either of bestriding the ridge or of moving on one of its sides with our hands lying over the top, as security against tumbling into the tarn on the left or into a frightful gully on the right, both of immense depth. Sometimes we thought it prudent to return; but that seemed unmanly and we proceeded thinking with Shakespeare that 'Dangers retreat when boldly they are confronted.'"

These terrifying descriptions in the guide books of the time obviously

Sharp Edge, Blencathra

reflected and probably affected the ordinary person's attitude to these wild places. Another account of an excursion of four people from Threlkeld to the summit of Blencathra describes how, as they climbed from the valley, one of the party was so *"astonished with the different appearance of objects in the valley beneath,"* that he chose to return home.

Before they had gone much further another of the four was suddenly taken ill and *"wished to lose blood to calm him down."* However he was persuaded to

46

Sharp Edge, Blencathra

continue as far as Scales Tarn where the party, now reduced to three, "*contemplated the scene with awestruck wonder.*" Not surprisingly perhaps, the potential blood letter refused to continue and was left at the tarn. His companions made their way to the summit up the steep slope to the south of Scales Tarn. On returning, by way of Sharp Edge, the narrator described his impressions as follows:

'We walked back by the side next to the lake, but to look down from thence was so terrible, I could not endure it a moment. We perceived from thence, that my companion, whom we had last left, was laid upon the ground; I pressed the guide to hasten to him, but he refused, alleging that a fog was rising, and it would be very hazardous for me to explore my way alone down the mountain: in a short time we were enveloped in a very dense vapour, so that we were obliged to keep near each other; the sudden change was almost incredible. It was with difficulty that my guide regained the passage, or dry bridge, which we missed on several attempts; and one incautious step would have plunged us into the horrid abyss.'

No further mention is made of the hapless bloodletter so I presume they met up with him on the way down. There was obviously a shortage of Mountain Leadership courses in those days. It goes without saying that you should not abandon people in distress half way up a mountain.

"On stern Blencartha's perilous height
The winds are tyrannous and strong;
And flashing forth unsteady light
From stern Blencartha's skiey height,
As loud the torrents throng!
Beneath the moon in gentle weather
They blend the earth and sky together.
But o! the sky and all her forms how quiet!
The things that seek the earth how full of
noise and riot!"
Coleridge

Blencathra in Winter

John Peel

Huntsman, made famous by a song

John Peel, the famous huntsman, was born at Park End in Caldbeck. The date of his birth is not known but he was baptised in St. Kentigern's Church, Caldbeck on the 24th September 1777. He fell in love, while still quite young, with Mary White of Uldale and they were to be wed. However, when the banns were called in church, her mother objected on the grounds:-

"Ther far ower yung"

John, however, was not to be so easily thwarted. Soon after, he followed the example of his parents before him, and eloped with Mary to Gretna Green on his mare *"Binsey,"* where they were wed over the blacksmith's anvil. Mrs White soon forgave them and, accepting the situation, endowed the couple with land worth several hundred pounds a year.

From then on John never looked back. He worked the land covered by the present Blencathra Foxhounds and soon built up a local reputation as a hunter of note. He hunted with his hounds at least twice a week, wearing his coat of *'gray'* made from the local Herdwick wool. It is often said that John Peel hunted on foot as do the Lakeland huntsmen of today. Undoubtedly he did hunt on foot at times, especially in his earlier years, but his greatest hunts were on horseback. Indeed John maintained his famous pack of twenty four hounds and two hunting horses for about fifty five years. John, unlike the huntsmen further south, did not hunt in scarlet as is depicted in some

portraits. Like his fellow Cumbrians, he wore a coat of *'Hodden Gray,'* often known locally as *'Skiddaw Gray.'* Even before his friend, John Graves, wrote the song that eventually immortalised his name, he became famous for his prowess as a huntsmen. He is reputed to have lived on a diet of porridge and milk for breakfast followed by only one other meal; of vegetables and meat, later in the afternoon. He must have been extremely fit to have run with the hounds over so many years. He often covered upwards of twenty miles in a day over very difficult country with its stone walls, peat

John Peel

bogs, undulating fields and craggy hills. In middle age John Peel became very friendly with John Woodcock Graves who, one winter night in 1832, whilst reminiscing with Peel, put pen to paper and wrote the now famous song. It was John's autobiography which included details of his friendship with Peel that provided the wealth of detail about how the song came to be written thus:-

"We were then both in the heyday of manhood, and hunters of the olden fashion; meeting the night before to arrange earth stopping, and in the morning to take the best part of the hunt - the drag over the mountains in the mist - while fashionable hunters still lay in the blankets. Large flakes of snow fell that evening. We sat by the fireside hunting over again many a good run, and recalling the feats of each particular hound, or narrow neck-break 'scapes, when a flaxen-haired daughter of mine came in saying, 'Father what do they say to what granny sings ?'
Granny was singing to sleep my eldest son - now a leading barrister in Hobart Town - with a very old rant called 'Bonnie (or Canny) Annie.'
The pen and ink for hunting appointments being on the table, the idea of writing a song to this old air forced itself upon me, and thus was produced, impromptu,
'D'ye ken John Peel with his coat so gray.'

When Peel heard the song he smiled, through a stream of tears, and John Graves jokingly said to him: 'Bye Jove, Peel, You'll be sung when were both run to earth.'
"

It was many years later however before the song became widely known in its present form. John Peel died at Ruthwaite, near Ireby, on Monday 13th November 1854. The song "D'ye ken John Peel" only became nationally famous after it was polished up, with Grave's approval, by one George Coward, who was preparing a book of "Songs and Ballads of Cumberland." The first verse and chorus of the song follow:

D' ye ken John Peel with his coat ..so gray ?
D' ye ken John Peel at the break of the day ?
D' ye ken John Peel when he's far, far a..way ?
With his hounds and his horn in the morn..ing ?
Twas the sound of his horn brought me from my bed.
And the cry of his hounds has me off..times led;
For Peel's view hol..loa would wa..ken the dead,
Or a fox from his lair in the morn..ing.

The Norse Influence

After the defeat of King Dunmail in the year 945 the Lakeland valleys became depopulated as many of his followers fled south into Wales. The Norsemen, who inhabited much of the coastal area and the Isle of Man, took advantage of this and encouraged the immigration of many of their countrymen into Lakeland. The young Norse farmers found this land of lakes and mountains very much to their liking and soon settled in, intermarrying with the local population. These incomers changed many of the mountain and valley names and possibly introduced the hardy Herdwick sheep to the area. The names of the places and valleys around Blencathra indicate that the indigenous Celts survived the invasions of the Angle and the Norsemen.

A document of 1278 relating to a dispute between Lord Thomas de Derwentwater and William de Threlkeld calls the river Glenderamakin by the name '*Glenermakan.*' McIntyre suggests that this is the Celtic '*Glyndyfr-Mcchyn;*' 'the river of the swine.' Similarly '*Glenderterra*' (Glenderterray in an old boundary role) looks like '*Glyndyfr-derw*' or Oak-dale river. The place names in the easily accessible and more fertile valleys such as at Threlkeld are undoubtedly Norse in origin. Threlkeld, for example, is from the Norse '*Thraela Kelda*' which means The '*Thralls*' or Bondsman's Well. The Norsemen soon worked their way higher into the country to establish their sheep runs. Thus we have Berrier (Bergherge in a document of 1166), the '*erghe*' or mountain pasture of the rocks. '*Scales*' is from '*skalar,*'(huts) and Bowscale from '*boll-skala,*' (farmstead huts). All of these lie on the lower slopes of Blencathra. It would appear, from the retention of the Celtic names in the more remote areas, that the Norse settlers allowed the British inhabitants to remain as serfs to work their farms.

Where did I come from?

Many of the Norse invaders had their coat of arms emblazoned onto their helmets and shields. A common feature of these was the emblem of a stork. Hence the stock answer from parents, that has come down through the generations, when their children asked the question above:

"The stork brought you, dear"

Those early Vikings were obviously very busy!!

Coat of Arms of the Storey family (Viking 'Storis')

Joseph Hawell
Herdwick Sheep Breeder

Canon H D Rawnsley in his book Lake Country Sketches (1903) writes of Joseph Hawell of Lonscale, who became well known as a Herdwick sheep breeder and, in his later years, as a Conservative and Unionist local politician. Indeed he used to say that he thought his father and mother '*had mixed a laal but yaller wid his poddish*' when he was a boy. At any rate he would have liked well enough to have branded his fleecy Skiddaw darlings with the words '*For King and Country,* ' and used a yellow'*dip*' if such had been in existence. Joseph was a Christmas present to the old oak cradle at Longlands Farm, for he was born on the 24th December 1854. Joseph grew up with his brothers to become as passionately fond of sheep as his father. His father had, from a present of ten gimmer lambs, given by his father when he was a young man, reared up a fine flock of 500 sheep on Frozen Fell and Wylie Ghyll, and of 300 at the back of Skiddaw.

Joseph Hawell

In 1869 the family moved from Uldale to Lonscales, between Saddleback and Skiddaw. Here they prospered, the success of the Hawells, father and sons, as breeders of pure Herdwicks being evidenced by the prizes and certificates that covered the walls from floor to ceiling. In 1891 the old man took ill from rheumatism, as shepherds often do. He was also troubled with asthma and, eventually, he had to take to his bed upstairs. Before he died he insisted on seeing one of his prize Herdwick rams and the sons had a tough job to get it to '*clim*' the '*stee*' and stand in the presence of the dying man.

Joseph married in 1886 and became well known not only for his sheepbreeding skills, but also for his interest in politics and his public speaking. His was a real patriot throwing his all into events such as building

Joseph Hawell

the bonfires on Skiddaw to celebrate the Royal Jubilee in 1887 and the tercentenary of the Armada in 1888. Unfortunately tragedy was to strike.

The Hawell monument on the Skiddaw track

Joseph was taken ill with influenza early in 1891 and simultaneously suffered a gum disease. His gum was lanced but the wound did not heal and within a day or two he was in bed, weak and delirious. He wanted to be up and about looking after his sheep, but on Friday, February 20th, *an angel came to the lonely farmstead of Lonscale,*

(Rawnsley's words) and Joseph died. He was 36 years old and left a wife and two young children. In reading through Joseph's correspondence after his death Rawnsley (who was a great family friend) came across a letter in which Joseph *'begs of a neighbour the loan of a horse and gear to enable him to bring down on a sledge from Lonscale Crag one of the finest single stones there.'* He wishes to set it up in some field on the farm, and have his father's name upon it and his father's deeds and prowess as a breeder of Herdwick sheep, with a single verse of descriptive poetry beneath, and he feels sure that his friend will lend a hand *'to erect a monument to at least one member of the Hawell family whose stainless, honourable, and straightforward life will always be pointed to with pride by his decendants.'* Canon

Rawnsley, along with others ensured that his wish was carried out. The memorial cross stands on the mountain path from Latrigg to Skiddaw and on it is carved, *'in symbol of eternity, the endless knot their Norse forefathers used.'*

Bishop of Barf

This white painted rock is clearly seen high up the scree on the lower slopes of Barf from the Swan Hotel in Thornthwaite. Tradition has it that in 1783 the newly appointed Bishop of Derry, now Londonderry, was in the area and stayed at the Swan. He apparently wagered that he would ride his horse up the side of Barf and onwards to the summit of Lord's Seat. Unfortunately, on attempting this feat, his horse fell on reaching the height of Bishop rock, killing both horse and rider. To commemorate this rather foolhardy enterprise the rock was painted white by patrons of the Swan, who still maintain the Bishop in his pristine white coat to this very day.

The Bishop Rock

The Bishop was laid to rest at the base of the mountain, now marked by the white painted rock known as the Bishop's Clerk. The fee paid to patrons painting the rock was set at one shilling and a quart of ale. According to the present landlord this is now negotiable. How true this tale is you must judge for yourself. In his book 'Mountain Ascents,' printed in 1886, John Barrow mentions the Bishop's Rock as *'standing apart and standing out well due to the fact it has been recently coated with whitewash.'* Although he stayed at the Swan he makes no mention of the story just related. What is sure is that the patrons of the Swan Hotel have kept the rock painted white for a very long time.

Embleton Sword

In the early part of the 19th century a Celtic sword, known as the 'Embleton

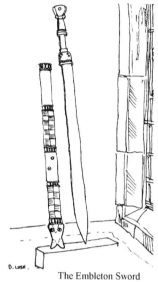
The Embleton Sword

Sword' was found in a field adjacent to Wythop Mill near the great stone, thought to be the site of an old battleground. The sword was in its sheath ornamented with enamels of various colours. The sword was placed in the Peter Crosthwaite Museum, Keswick, but it eventually found its way to the British Museum. The sword is believed to date from the year 50 BC and is probably the best example of its kind in Britain. In 1985, on hearing that the sword was miles from its ancestral home, three apprentices at Workington's British Steel Plant determined to make a steel replica of it. The sword was forged by the apprentices and the scabbard was made and decorated by Mrs P Beaty of Cockermouth. In April of that year, the replica sword, a truly beautiful object, was handed over to the village at a ceremony in St. Cuthbert's Church, where it now resides.

Hermit of Skiddaw

Skiddaw can boast a hermit as can various other hills in the district. About 1864 a Scotsman from Banffshire, one George Smith, came to the mountain and built himself a hut on a ledge of Skiddaw Dodd, now covered by Dodd Wood. McIntyre describes how George, in order to enter his lair, had to climb a wall and then drop down through a hole into the interior of the dwelling. His table was a stone and he slept on a bed of leaves. He wore no hat, coat or shoes, washed his single shirt in the water of the beck and let it dry upon his back. He frequently ate his meals uncooked, and was so partial to whisky that he sometimes found himself in the hands of the police. His ostensible means of livelihood was the painting of portraits, but as he often refused payment for these, his survival was somewhat of a mystery. Alas, his home was eventually destroyed by the nineteenth century version of our 'yobs' and George went to live in Keswick. He suffered from religious mania, however, and was finally removed to an asylum in his native Banffshire, where he most probably died.

The Pride of Lorton Vale

Wordsworth wrote:-

"There is a Yew tree, pride of Lorton Vale,
Which to this day stands single, in the midst
of its own darkness,as it stood of yore.
Of vast circumference and gloom profound.
This solitary tree! a living thing,
Produced too slowly ever to decay;
Of form and aspect too magnificent
To be destroyed."

In 1898 Edmund Bogg described the tree as being *"now only a wreck of its former glory."* He continues: *"In its pride and strength the trunk measured twenty four feet in circumference; one of its own branches was some years ago wrenched off right down to the ground. At another time the tree was actually sold for fifteen pounds to a cabinet maker from Whitehaven, and two men began to stub it up, but fortunately a gentleman from Cockermouth, hearing of its proposed destruction, made overtures to the owner, and thus preserved, though shorn of its ancient dignity, the pride of Lorton Vale."*

The Lorton Yew

The tree can still be seen today on the green behind the village hall in High Lorton. Its present condition is much better than that depicted in this drawing from Edmund Bogg's Book, published in 1898.

Incidentally the large barn-like building which is now the village hall was originally a bobbin mill and later a well known local brewery now based in Cockermouth.

55

The Beauty of Buttermere
the story of Mary Robinson

Mary Robinson, known as 'The Beauty of Buttermere,' became famous in the late 18th century as a result of an account given of her by the author of "A Fortnight's Ramble to the Lakes in Westmorland, Lancaster and Cumberland" (1792), see below. Unfortunately this brought her to the attention of one John Hatfield, a dashing rogue and impostor, who left a trail of unpaid bills and fraudulent transactions wherever he went. John, later known as the Keswick impostor, took up residence at the Queen's Head Keswick in July 1802. He then proceeded to woo Mary, the innkeeper's daughter at Buttermere, and eventually married her using the assumed name of Alexander Augustus Hope, brother of the Earl of Hopetoun. The wedding took place at Lorton Church on October 2nd 1802, the groom having concealed the fact that he already had a wife and two children at Tiverton.

Mary Robinson

Alas, soon afterwards, his crimes caught up with him. The notice of his wedding in a Scottish newspaper brought his debtors on his trail. He was arrested, arraigned at Carlisle and sentenced to death for forgery. Even in those times this penalty was considered to be exceptionally harsh and, not surprisingly, he appealed. There was widespread public sympathy for his plight but the expected reprieve was not forthcoming and John Hatfield was publicly hanged at the Sands, Carlisle, on Saturday September 3rd 1803. Mary, who by this time was expecting a child, eventually got over this experience. She was married to a local statesman and lived to a ripe old age (see later). Contemporary accounts of the hanging, which took place on the island between Eden Bridges at Carlisle, describe John's perfect manners and bravery as he calmly accepted his fate:

The Beauty of Buttermere
The hanging of John Hatfield

"*As soon as the carriage door had been opened by the under-sheriff, he alighted with his two companions. A small dung-cart, boarded over, had been placed under the gibbet, and a ladder was placed against it, which he instantly ascended. He was dressed in a black jacket, black silk waistcoat, fustian pantaloons, shoes and white cotton stockings. He was perfectly cool and collected. At the same time, his conduct displayed nothing of levity, of insensibility, or of hardihood. He was more anxious to give proof of resignation than of heroism. His countenance was extremely pale, but his hand never trembled. He immediately untied his neck handkerchief, and placed a bandage over his eyes. Then he desired the hangman, who was extremely awkward, to be as expert as possible about it, and that he would wave a handkerchief when he was ready. The hangman, not having fixed the rope in its proper place, he put up his hand and turned it himself. Then he requested the jailer would step on the platform and pinion his arms a little harder saying that, when he had lost his senses, he might attempt to lift them to his neck. The rope was completely fixed about five minutes before five o'clock: it was slack, and he merely said, 'May the Allmighty bless you all.' Nor did he falter in the least, when he tied the cap, shifted the rope, and took the handkerchief from his neck. Having taken leave of the jailer and sheriff, he prepared himself for his fate. He was at this time heard to exclaim, 'My spirit is strong, though my body is weak.' Great apprehensions were entertained that it would be necessary to tie him up a second time. The noose slipped twice, and he fell down about eighteen inches. His feet at last were almost touching the ground, but his excessive weight, which occasioned this accident, speedily relieved him from pain. He expired in a moment and without any struggle .*"

The Life of John Hatfield (1846).

Dramatic as this true life situation was, the popular press at the time had to embellish it. About 1841 a novel was published in three volumes for the circulating library entitled "James Hatfield and the Beauty of Buttermere" by Robert Cruickshank. The description of the hero's demise in the novel illustrates the free use of artistic licence in these matters. According to the novel, John (James in the book) was accompanied to the scaffold by his friend Mr Fenton; the curate of Lorton. Mr Fenton, overcome with the situation, promptly collapsed and died. As he fell to the ground he was caught and supported by the hangman's victim. This of course brought cries from the crowd for the hanging to be stopped, as it was obviously a sign from heaven.

The Beauty of Buttermere

To no avail. As the trapdoor dropped, Mary appeared, distraught, at the foot of the scaffold.

Apparently this story still has an appeal today. Only recently the Cumbrian author Melvyn Bragg has written a novel around this tale.

There follows an extract from a Lakeland guide, first published in 1792, in which the author, Joseph Budsworth, describes his first encounter with the girl who was to become known as 'The Beauty of Buttermere.' In his book Mary is referred to as 'Sally of Buttermere.'

"Her mother and she were spinning woollen yarn in the back kitchen; on our going into it, the girl flew away as swift as a mountain sheep, and it was not until our return from Scale Force, that we could say we first saw her; she brought in part of our dinner, and seemed to be about fifteen. Her hair was thick and long, of a dark brown, and though unadorned with ringlets, did not seem to want them; her face was a fine contour, with full eyes, and lips as red as vermillion; her cheeks had more of the lily than the rose and although she had never been out of the village, (and, I hope, will have no ambition to wish it) she had a manner about her which seemed better calculated to set off dress, than dress her. She was a very Lavinia, "seeming when unadorn'd, adorn'd the most." When we first saw her at her distaff, after she had got the better of her first fears, she looked an angel, and I doubt not but she is the "reigning lily" of the valley."

(A Rambler, 1792)

Although this story is well known, possibly due to the fact that it was written of at the time by Wordsworth and others, little was recorded of what happened to Mary afterwards. Mary's later life has recently been revealed by the Caldbeck Local History Society in their publication 'Caldbeck Characters'. Sometime after returning to work with her parents at the Fish Inn, Buttermere she met Richard Harrison, son of a well - established farming

Todcrofts farm, Caldbeck

family from Caldbeck. They were married at Brigham in 1808 and took over the family farm of Todcrofts, while Richard's parents moved to Upton Gate. They had seven children and apparently lived a happy life at Caldbeck. Mary died in 1837, followed by her husband in 1853.

Deaths in a Flood at Loweswater

There have been many lives lost over the years in the district due to both natural and man-made calamities. One such happening at Loweswater was recounted by Edmund Bogg in 1902:

Loweswater and Crabtree Beck

"Many years ago a small reservoir, or tarn, on the hill above the lake, burst, and came rolling in one huge wave towards the lake; a farm stood in its path, and one of the occupants, a girl who was outside the house, saw the dark mass of water sweeping downwards. Darting into the house, she informed the inmates (the master and a female) of the occurrence. These two had just reached the outside of the door in their endeavour to escape, when the wave caught them both, swept them into the lake, and their bodies were never discovered, whilst strange to say, the girl, who was first to discover the inundation, was saved by the water forcibly banging the door in her face and holding her prisoner, when she was in the act of following the other persons."

The small dam was across Crabtree Beck and provided water for Loweswater lead mine which is situated in Kirkhill Wood, immediately west of the Kirkstile Inn.

Cruelty to Animals in the 1790's

Unfortunately cruelty to our domestic animals is not a new phenonemon. In the book mentioned above the author describes his visit to Scale Force

Scales Force

Waterfall. He recounts that they saw local people hurling dogs over the 172 ft fall for 'sport.' He and his party were most disturbed at this and urged the locals to desist. This, thankfully, they did whilst expressing surprise because other visitors had previously enjoyed the spectacle. It was apparently laid on as a spectator sport for visitors. His moving account of how the poor wretched creatures (those that survived the fall) "limped away looking bewildered at the treatment they had received from their owners," showed a compassion that was sadly lacking in the local Buttermere folk.

The Secret Valley and the Battle of Rannerdale

In the 1920's Nicholas Size, novellist, local historian and later innkeeper came to the Bridge Hotel, Buttermere. He had fallen in love with Lakeland and its history, particularly the area around Buttermere. It was in 1930 that his book 'The Secret Valley' was first published. This is a fact/fiction novel in which the characters and events were essentially accurate, but the detail was embroidered in to make the history come alive. It gives a fascinating insight into the attempts by the early English/Norse settlers to resist the Saxon and later the Norman attempts to conquer this mountain kingdom. I have attempted below to bring the essentials of this story to you in the manner of Nicholas Size.

As stated earlier in the section on 'Norse Influence' many Norwegian settlers came to this land in the years following King Dunmail's defeat at Dunmail Raise. They were wary of Saxon attack and so set about defending their mountain land from the southern English. To this end the great Norse commander Olaf Tryggvesson, was asked to come and advise about the

The Buttermere Valley

defence of their country. Olaf surveyed the land from the top of Gavel (Great Gable), and saw a valley which was almost impregnable (The Buttermere Valley). Its best means of access was by boat along Crummock Water. All other access points are by high passes, which would be easy to defend. The Norwegians built fortifications at the foot of the lake to act as a depot for food storage etc.. (The ground plan of these fortifications are still supposed to be visible). The supplies could then be ferried down the lake by boat as needed.

However the Saxon attack never came and it was nearly 100 years later, after the Norman Conquest, that their preparations proved necessary. About the year 1070 Boethar the Younger, a grandson of the leader who had taken Olaf's advice, decided to make this hidden valley his base from where they could command the defence of Lakeland. It was only much later that the lake and valley became known as *Boethar*mere or Buttermere. Together with his brother Ackin, Earl Boethar (*Jarl* in the old Norse, meaning warrior king)

The Secret Valley

set about fortifying their secret valley. Earl Boethar regularly organised attacks on the Norman convoys as they passed up Lonsdale and down the Eden Valley. They were very successful as the Normans were fighting in country which did not suit them. The booty of war, armour for man and horse, provided even more resources for the local people. We must remember that the local shepherds and farmers would be as fit as our modern fell runners and would know the mountains intimately. They could travel easily and quickly over terrain that would be impossible for the Norman soldiers. As a result small detachments of Normans would be massacred, whenever they ventured away from safety.

The Cumbrians were superior in their archery as well. Earl Boethar had brought back the idea of the longbow from his earlier years spent in Pembrokeshire and they quickly developed it until it could fire arrows twice

as far as the more rapid firing Norman short bow (which eventually became the cross-bow). The increased speed of use of the Norman bow was of little help in guerilla warfare. The Norman soldiers were also superstitious and the small bands of wild men that appeared out of the mountain mists terrified them.

A famous warrior of this time was old Ari Knudson, who devastated many a Norman convoy. He ventured into the wild country between Brough and Alston and often organised raids in unexpected places. People to this day still use the phrase 'Fighting like old Harry', so his fame is still not dead after about 900 years.

Eventually the Normans retaliated. Using Penrith and Lowther castles for a base, an overwhelming army of horse and foot, led by Ranulf Meschin, attacked the broad valley running from Threlkeld to Keswick and established themselves south of Keswick at Castle Crag. This they fortified with stockades and earthworks.

At last Ranulf made a very definite move by marching the bulk of his army round to Stair in Newlands, where a camp was made. Keeping Derwentwater on their left they fought their way round to Littletown. Here they were confronted by four valleys. All were well defended and none knew which to

The Secret Valley

take. They set up camp, sleeping fearfully with their arms, where Newlands Church now stands. As Armand de Fe'camp, the deputy commander, settled his camp that night he had no idea that, when his enemies had fallen back that day from Catbells, their retreat had been controlled from a ridge on his right (now called Aikin Knott, on Ard Crags) and that a very large force of men had been kept deliberately out of sight, so that he might spend the night in a convenient position for his enemies. In the middle of the night amidst a downpour of rain, the whole countryside seemed to come to life. Thousands of well-armed men, without lights, gathered on every side, attacked the sleeping camp, turning it into a slaughter house. The first Newlands Church was erected afterwards to mark the place where this Norman army died.

Ranulf was still at Keswick but his deputy was killed. Of the few who escaped none could say much other than 'a million men or demons had swept over them in the dark and then vanished'.

The Cumbrians, making the best of their advantage, were pressing up Borrowdale to cut him off from Penrith so he was forced to withdraw along the Roman road which runs along the east side of Bassenthwaite to Spatrie (modern Aspatria). Here the remains of his army joined that of his brother William in territory that had already been conquered and fortified.

This led to even greater preparations than before to defeat Earl Boethar. Papcastle, near Cockermouth, was occupied in force and regiments were withdrawn from Carlisle, Kendal and all the castles of the Eden valley. Together with new troops from Normandy they put together an army more suited to the conquest of Scotland than Lakeland.

The Normans under the command of Ranulf Meschin crossed the Derwent near where Cockermouth Castle now stands and, in spite of many attacks particularly at night, they established control over these flat lands.

Everyone knew that eventually their valley would be attacked from the north and a plan had been set up to foil this. The road in those times went up over the shoulder of Rannerdale Knotts to the east of Hause Point (the route of the present road, blasted out in more recent times). This route was obscured by removing all of the road material down to the bare rock, so that there was no obvious way up that way. The Earl then created a new well-marked path, further to the left, winding up Rannerdale Valley and still traceable near the top. This road went nowhere, but would lead the unsuspecting Normans up the narrow valley, which was hemmed in on both sides by crags perfect for ambush. Defences further up the valley at Brackenthwaite, under Whiteside, were also strengthened to make the Normans passage south even more

The Battle of Rannerdale

difficult. The Normans marched south from Cockermouth on a cloudless summer day. As they proceeded they were harried by English archers with their longbows, mounted on pack ponies, so that they could easily keep out of range of the Norman crossbows, but exact a high toll of the advancing Normans.

At Lorton the Normans halted for two nights and a day, which was spent exploring the Whinlatter Pass and posting bodies of archers at strategic points, so that on the second day Ranulf felt it safe to move on again.

In the afternoon the battle commenced at Brackenthwaite where all sorts of earthworks had been made, but the Normans heavy cavalry was irresistable, in spite of the all of the efforts of the English.

As a result of this battle six burial places were subsequently built to accommodate the corpses (Cornhow, Picket How, Palace How, Turner Howe, Backhows and Brackenthwaite How). It was an expensive victory for the Normans. The English mostly escaped into Lanthwaite Woods or up Gasgale Gill onto Coledale Hause, from where they could march home via Whiteless Pike in a couple of hours and those in the woods were ferried down the lake. Ranulf decided to press on immediately the next day, while his troops were flush with victory, rather than suffer several nights of guerilla attacks from the surrounding lake and fells.

The Normans approached Rannerdale, being led by the mounted English archers, still harrying them but keeping themselves out of range of the Norman arrows. Unknown to the Normans, the pick of the English army lay just round the Hause at Rannerdale and they could have held the point against the whole Norman host if it had tried to get round or over it by the old route. The Normans examined the lake near the point, saw it was deep water and decided that the only danger would be from English who could get round by boat, so left a dozen or so men as a guard. The rocks in front of them were steep and bare and they were harassed from above by a few archers on the Knotts. Gradually they edged round into Rannerdale, following the English archers up the new track. The English appeared to be losing the appetite for battle. Elaborate earthworks near the entrance to Rannerdale were easily captured and overrun. Soon Ranulf and the majority of his army were well within the valley of Rannerdale and it became apparent that the English were going to make a stand further up.

Suddenly an outcry was heard from the rear. Earl Ackin (the brother of Boethar) with thousands of well-armed men, had descended the rocks, or had been put round the point by boat, so that a swarm of them had charged

The Battle of Rannerdale

through the camp followers, and occupied an earthwork, being joined by men from the opposite side of the valley. They were already pressing forward so as to cramp and crush the Normans into one anothers way. Simultaneously the English on all sides threw themselves into the attack thus the Normans became massed together, not knowing what to do next.

Loud horns then sounded and at different points well - armed and armoured men fell into the Norse formation like a spear head and pushed forward among the Normans, left handed men to the left and right handed men to the right, with champion axe wielders at the apex of each spearhead.

Ranulf decided to get out of the valley and sounded the retirement, his formations became reversed and everything was blocked. The spearheads did their work. The archers on the ridge were reinforced by women and poured arrows into the mass, while from the slopes of Whiteless Pike and Grasmoor fearless men poured down into the fray.

Earl Boethar was on the ridge directing the battle and soon he unleashed his final weapon against the Normans. A crowd of wild berserkers, rushed down the slopes, and made particularly for the horses of the Norman Knights. These berserkers were half drunk with spirit which made them impervious to pain. They were fast and lightly armed and wherever they could they slipped in and made for the big horses, which they disembowelled as they passed beneath their bellies. A complete route followed. Ranulf escaped to Lorton and then Cockermouth.

No further attempts were made to conquer Earl Boethar and Lakeland was at peace until King Stephen (1135 - 1154), in his attempts to buy friends, ceded it to Scotland together with Carlisle and the Eden Valley. Ackin, the brother of Boethar was killed in the battle and laid to rest where the little chapel was subsequently built in Rannerdale. Later his body was moved to where he had commanded his great victory in Newlands, Ackin Howe, now called Aikin Knott on modern maps.

Newlands Church with
Aikin Knott in the left
background